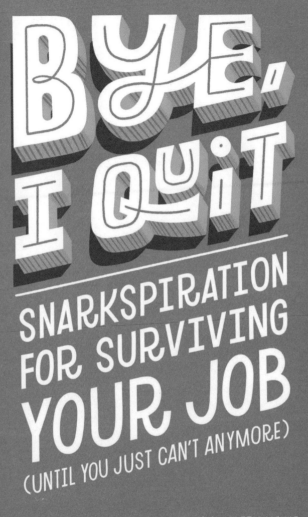

BYE, I QUIT

SNARKSPIRATION FOR SURVIVING YOUR JOB

(UNTIL YOU JUST CAN'T ANYMORE)

WITH CHARMING ILLUSTRATIONS BY FAITH HENKE

HARPER
Celebrate

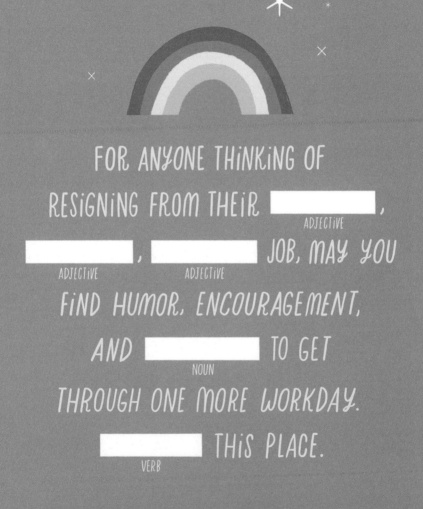

FOR ANYONE THINKING OF RESIGNING FROM THEIR _____,
ADJECTIVE

_____, _____ JOB, MAY YOU
ADJECTIVE   ADJECTIVE

FIND HUMOR, ENCOURAGEMENT,

AND _____ TO GET
NOUN

THROUGH ONE MORE WORKDAY.

_____ THIS PLACE.
VERB

YOU ARE MORE THAN JUST YOUR JOB

THE THREE MOST
BEAUTIFUL WORDS IN
THE ENGLISH LANGUAGE:

THREE. DAY. WEEK.

THE NEW

CONDES

WEEKEN

ENTRY-LEVEL JOBS THAT

THE PA

OUTDATED

MICROMAN

LACK OF REM

NSFW

CENSION

D WORK

AREN'T ENTRY LEVEL

Y GAP

DRESS CODES

AGEMENT

OTE OPTIONS

REASON NOT TO QUIT TODAY:

THE COWORKER WHO BAKES

THINGS THAT ARE WORTH CRYING OVER	THINGS THAT AREN'T WORTH CRYING OVER
· THE BEGINNING OF *UP*	· YOUR BOSS
· SEASONAL ALLERGIES	
· THE ENDING OF *IT'S A WONDERFUL LIFE*	
· PUPPIES IN RAIN BOOTS	
· YOUR BEST FRIEND'S WEDDING	
· STUBBING YOUR TOE	

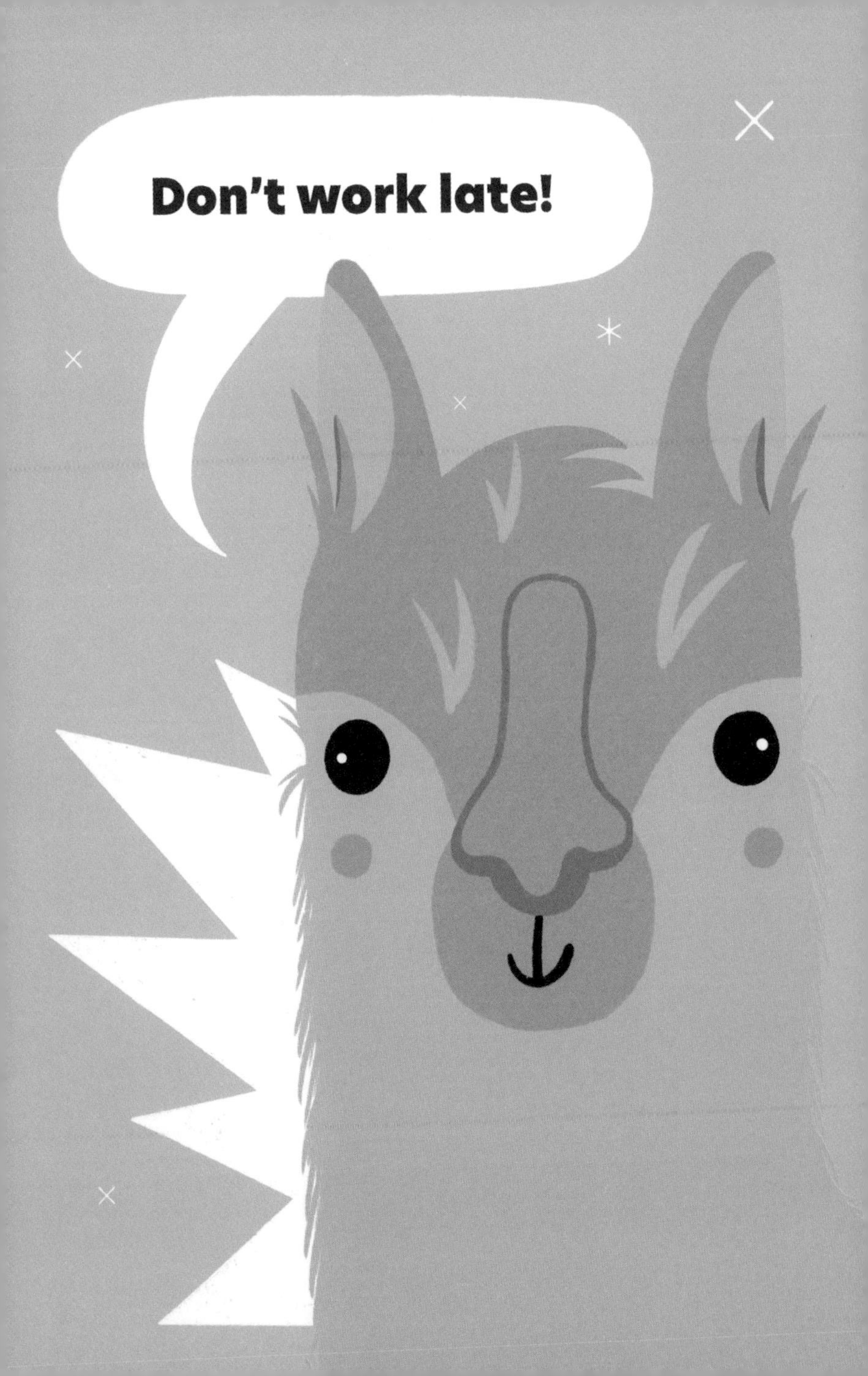
Don’t work late!

**Never trouble another
for what you can do yourself—
like making a decent pot of coffee
for the break room.**

Some days call for

On a scale of one
to CVS receipts,
how long is your
to-do list today?

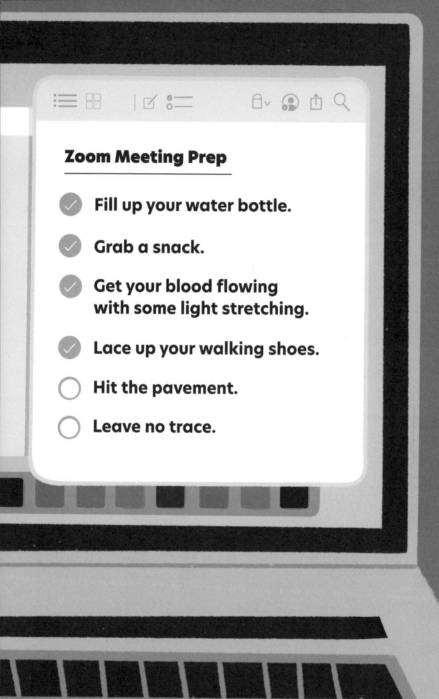

EVERYTHING THAT NEEDS TO GET DONE WILL GET DONE.

"If you don't know where you are going, any road will get you there."

—*Lewis Carroll*

Should you send that passive-aggressive email?

DID SOMEONE EAT YOUR LUNCH OUT OF THE OFFICE FRIDGE?

YES

NO

DO YOU KNOW WHO IT WAS?

DON'T DO IT.

NO

YES

HAVE THEY DONE IT BEFORE?

AN EXCUSE
FOR A TWO-HOUR
TACO LUNCH.

OH, IT IS <u>ON</u>.

NO

YES

OKAY.
WAS IT TACOS?

COULD HAVE BEEN
AN HONEST MIX-UP.
LUNCH SWAP?

DOES IT MATTER?

NO

HOW GOOD
WAS THE LUNCH?

YES

Let's get tipsy.

8:59 A.M. LOGiN:

REPEAT AFTER ME.

TODAY WiLL BE GREAT.

TODAY WiLL BE GREAT.

TODAY WiLL BE GREAT.

TODAY WiLL BE GREAT.

9:00 A.M. MEETiNG:

I STAND CORRECTED.

Did you get to shower,
eat breakfast, and
make it to work today?

You are—
and this cannot be stressed enough—
a sensation.

**Did you know weekend work emails
are illegal in France?
Close the computer and eat a croissant.**

The one constant
in life and work
is change.

Dessert Pairings for Every Kind of Meeting

LAST-MINUTE REQUEST

THEY JUST SAID THAT OUT LOUD?

WE'VE ALREADY TALKED ABOUT THIS

ENDING RIGHT WHERE YOU STARTED

EVERYONE'S TALKING ABOUT THEIR WEEKEND

SUCKING UP TO THE BOSS

COULD HAVE BEEN AN EMAIL

WELL, THAT WAS SUPER PRODUCTIVE

Lady Gaga wrote
"Born This Way" in ten minutes.

Elton John and Bernie Taupin wrote
"Your Song" in twenty minutes.

Lorde wrote "Royals" in thirty minutes.

Dolly Parton wrote
"Jolene" and "I Will Always Love You"
in a single day.

THE BEST WORK SHOWS UP WHEN YOU NEED IT.

**Some days you're the Oscars
and some days you're the Razzies.**

Either way, you're a star.

RECIPE FOR A REALLY GOOD FRIDAY

TAKEOUT FROM YOUR
FAVORITE LUNCH SPOT

AFTERNOON RETAIL THERAPY

WEEKEND BRUNCH
RESERVATIONS

ONE PAIR OF
COMFY SWEATPANTS

3-4 LISTENS OF
"JUST GOT PAID" BY *NSYNC

INSTRUCTIONS: BAKE UNTIL 5:00 P.M.
AND SERVE IMMEDIATELY.

Cold Brew

1. BREW A CUP OF COFFEE.

2. SIT DOWN AT YOUR DESK.

3. TACKLE YOUR TO-DO LIST, GET PULLED INTO THREE MEETINGS, PUT OUT A COUPLE OF QUICK FIRES, ANSWER YOUR EMAILS, WATCH YOUR INBOX FILL UP, START FEELING HUNGRY, LOOK AT THE TIME, AND SEE THAT IT'S 1:00 P.M.

4. YOUR COFFEE IS NOW COLD.

5. ADD ICE.

6. CONGRATULATIONS.

Cheers to the
coworkers who make
each day better.

**Hey, you.
Do something nice for yourself today.**

Busy Day Check-In

- Take a deep breath.
- Raise your shoulders.
- Drop them.
- Stretch your arms up to the ceiling and float them down.
- Do that again. And again.
- Do it faster.
- Keep flapping.
- Fly home, little bird.

**Stan Lee created his first
Marvel superhero when he was 40.**

**Julia Child wrote her first cookbook
when she was 50.**

**Colonel Sanders franchised
his business at age 65.**

**Noah Webster completed
An American Dictionary of the English Language
when he was 66.**

You have time.

Whatever they're paying you,
it's not enough.

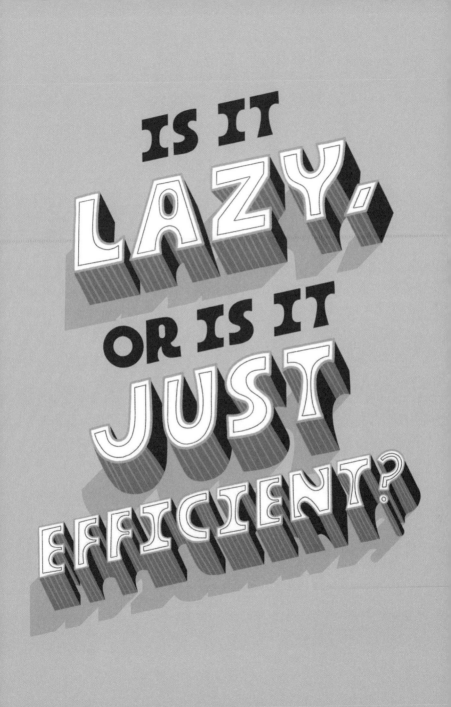

RECIPE FOR GETTING MOTIVATED

FAVORITE POWER BLAZER

1 STRONG CUP OF COFFEE

A WALK IN THE SUNSHINE

THE *ROCKY* THEME SONG

INCONSPICUOUS
CHAIR DANCING

A VACATION VISION BOARD

INSTRUCTIONS: MIX TOGETHER AND SERVE GENEROUS PORTIONS.

You've accomplished
enough today.
Pet a dog.

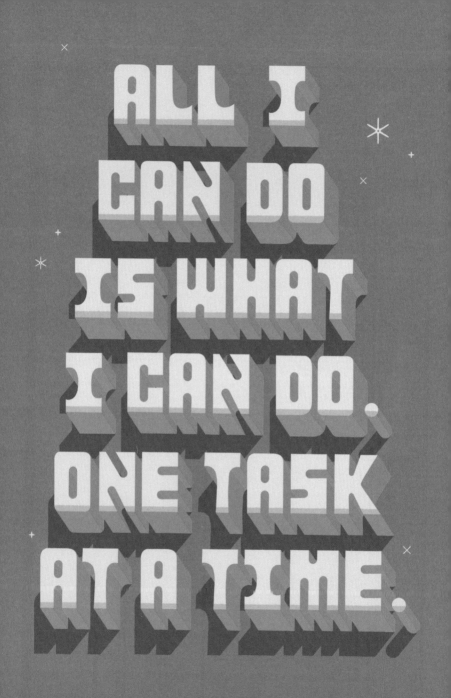

Make These Illegal in the Office

- Loud chewing
- Microwaved broccoli
- Burnt popcorn
- Gum popping
- Fish!!!

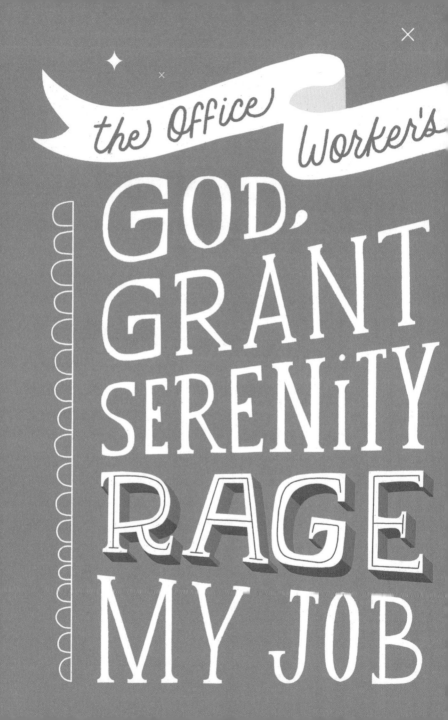

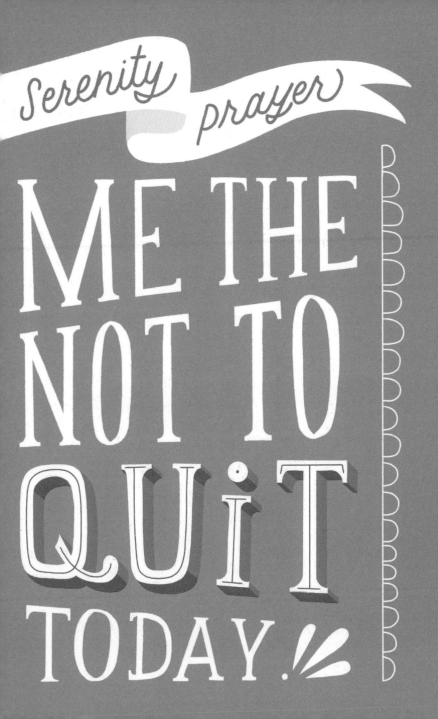

REASON NOT TO QUIT TODAY:

THE MANAGER
WHO ALWAYS
HEARS
YOU

Monday, 7:00 a.m.

"How about if I sleep a little bit longer and forget all this nonsense?"

—Franz Kafka, *The Metamorphosis*

Power Colors to Wear for Every Occasion

Rocking your
presentation

Negotiating
your salary

Undercutting
your office nemesis

Drinks with your
happy hour posse

Schmoozing
clients

Lunch with
your work crush

Kissing up
to your boss

First day
of your job

Last day
of your job

TO:

FROM:

Hello,

You've reached me outside of work hours. I am not sorry I missed your email, as I value my free time and work-life balance.

Good day.

SAVE

I WILL NOT FEEL GUILTY FOR TAKING MY WELL-EARNED TIME OFF.

few things in life bring us together like the shared hatred of a bad tipper.

TOUCAN
DO THiS!

Meetings after 5:00 p.m.
Meetings before 9:00 a.m.
Meetings during lunch.

Some days you're a
Leslie Knope.

Some days you're a
Ron Swanson.

Be an Ann Perkins today.

NORMALiZE

lunch
naps.

When Weekend Work Is Acceptable

 NEVER

"LEARN FROM YESTERDAY, LIVE FOR TODAY, HOPE FOR TOMORROW. THE IMPORTANT THING IS NOT TO STOP QUESTIONING."

ALBERT EINSTEIN

Gift Guide for Your Work Wife

CHOCOLATE

spa lala

relax

GIFT CARD FOR FACIAL

A NEW PAIR
OF ZOOM PJ'S

A HAPPY HOUR KIT
DELIVERED TO HER HOUSE

A JAR OF YOUR TEARS
CANCELING YOUR MEETING
Let's reschedule our meeting for next week.
PLANE TRIP TO PERU

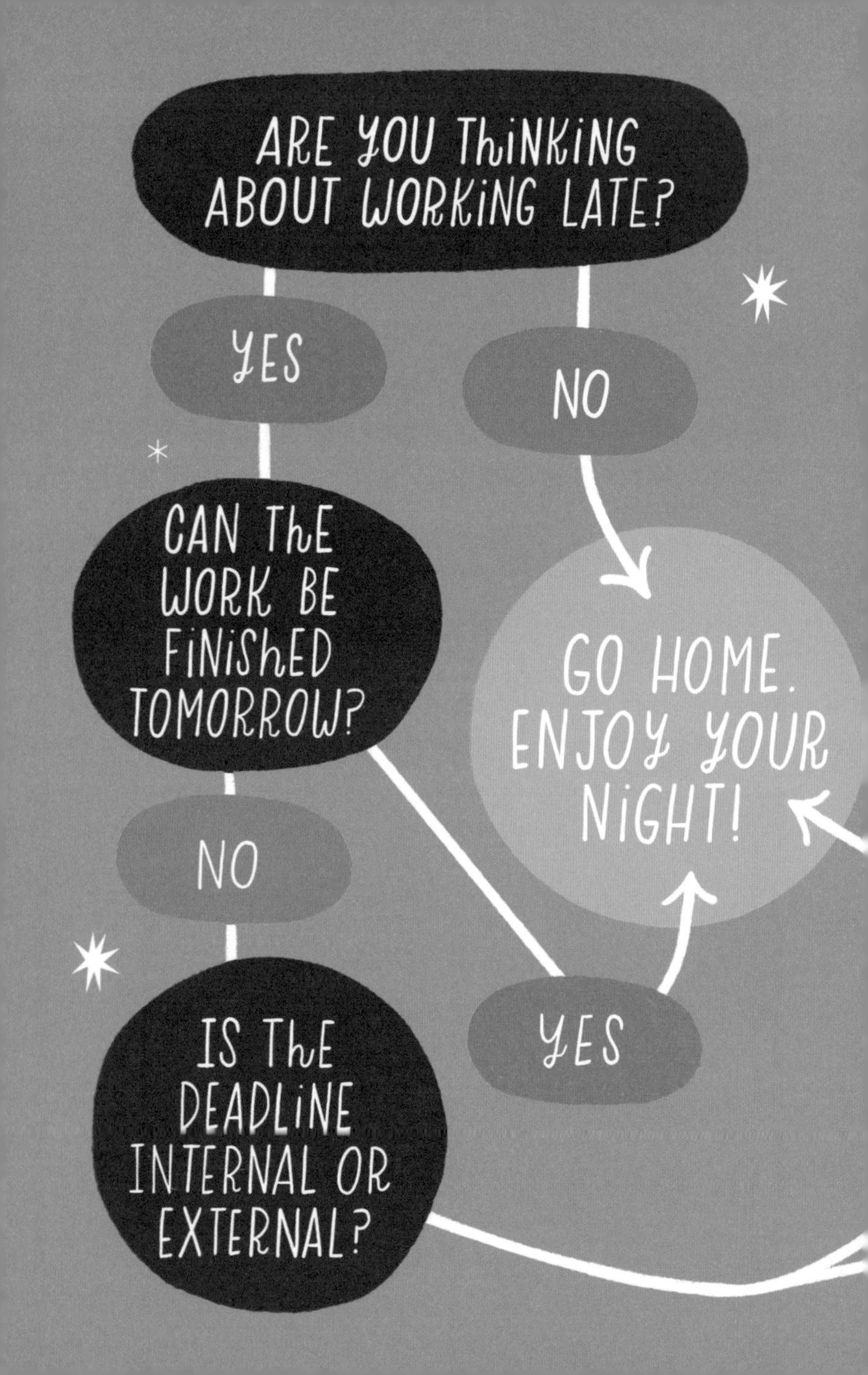
ARE YOU THINKING ABOUT WORKING LATE?
YES
NO
CAN THE WORK BE FINISHED TOMORROW?
GO HOME. ENJOY YOUR NIGHT!
NO
YES
IS THE DEADLINE INTERNAL OR EXTERNAL?

RESPOND THAT YOU'LL GET TO IT TOMORROW.
ALRIGHT. JUST THIS ONCE. ADD SNACKS.
YES
NO
DID SOMEONE DROP THIS IN YOUR LAP WITHOUT ANY NOTICE?
INTERNAL
EXTERNAL

YOU DESERVE A BREAK

PEOPLE NOT RESPONDING
TO YOUR REQUESTS:
DOUBLE MARGS AT HAPPY HOUR

RUDE CUSTOMER:
TWO-HOUR COFFEE BREAK

VAGUE MEETING REQUEST
FROM YOUR BOSS:
SPA DAY

PASSED UP FOR PROMOTION:
SWiSS ALPS

UNATTAiNABLE DEADLiNE:
ARCTiC CRUiSE

UNDERCUT iN PUBLiC:
REMOTE iSLAND

Steps to Cope When One of the Good Ones Quits First

---

1. Cry.

2. Pour a glass of wine.

3. Try to make new friends at work.

4. Give up on making new friends at work.

5. More wine.

6. Cry again.

7. Eat a sandwich.

8. Update your résumé.

9. Get a new job.

10. Toast to a new you.

**There isn't a bucket big enough
to bail out this shipwreck.**

Get out while you can.

PASSIVE-AGGRESSIVE SECRET SANTA GUIDE

FOR THE ONE WHO'S ALWAYS LATE ON DEADLINE

FOR THE ONE WHO BRINGS A SMELLY LUNCH

FOR THE ONE WHO'S LATE TO MEETINGS

FOR THE ONE WHO PLAYS THEIR MUSIC TOO LOUD

FOR THE ONE WHO
WALKS AROUND
TOO MUCH

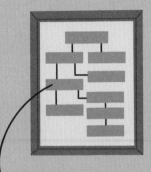

FOR THE ONE WHO
FORGETS YOUR NAME

FOR THE ONE
WHO OVERSHARES

FOR THE ONE WHO
CAN'T TAKE A JOKE